This notebook belongs to:

Made in the USA
Monee, IL
29 November 2022

19015088R00073